AuthorHouse™
1663 Liberty Drive
Bloomington, IN 47403
www.authorhouse.com
Phone: 833-262-8899

This book is printed on acid-free paper.

ISBN: 978-1-6655-4145-9 (sc)
ISBN: 978-1-6655-4147-3 (hc)
ISBN: 978-1-6655-4146-6 (e)

Print information available on the last page.

Published by AuthorHouse 02/19/2022

author HOUSE®

The
first time I
knew God
was real

It's Sunday morning, and my mom knocks on the door and tells me to rise and shine. As I struggle to get up, I hear the radio playing her favorite song, Wake Up Everybody by Teddy Pendergrass; it's blasting but a sure way to get us up.

My brother and I race downstairs for breakfast as we fall into our chairs.

Dad begins to pray over breakfast; we hurry to eat, so we're not late for bible school. Later that evening, Mom asked if we enjoyed bible school? And if we learned anything? I said, of course, mom, God loves us and smiled. She gives both my brother and me a kiss good night.

Before leaving our rooms, she instructs us to say our prayers because we are blessed to have a roof over our heads and then reminds us that we will know God is real and present. I smile again, tell her good night, and then say the prayer my dad taught me.

Now I lay me down to sleep, I pray to God my soul to keep, If I should die before I wake, I pray to God my soul to take, If I should live for another day, I pray to God to guide my way, then I say goodnight.

Every night, this happens; my parents would first go to my younger brothers' room, then stop by mine, always letting us know that we are loved and making sure that we have said our prayers.

It's the last day of school, and I'm reminding my dad that he has to sign me up for Parks and Rec, so that I can play baseball this year. The following two weeks go by fast, my mom tells me that she received a call from Coach Miller, stating that I will be playing on the Blue Bears team this summer.

I run over to her excitedly and give her a big hug; she smiles at me and says, you know, you have to start practicing if you want to be a good player.

The team and I practiced for weeks, and now we're competing against other teams, it's way more exciting, stressful and intimidating than I ever expected, but I'm not a quitter and endure the bumps and bruises.

It's thirteen of us on the team: Christian, Josiah, Landon, Michael, Alex, Jaden, Nash, Aiden, Auden, Sean, Preston, Ricky, and me, MJ.

As luck would have it, the Blue Bears made it to the playoffs, our record 10-2, and we could not be happier. It's Monday, one week before the championship game, the team is meeting the Coach to find out who we will be playing. We are all thrilled until the Coach informed us that we will be playing the Mighty Hawks.

We look at each other and you know without a doubt that we're scared, because the Mighty Hawks have not lost a game all summer. The Coach tells us to calm our fears and adds, we will play the Mighty Hawks like we play all of our opponents, with pride, confidence and teamwork.

Immediately we knew the Coach was right and quickly began cheering for our team; huddled together we felt strength and courage in ourselves and gave one another high-fives.

Today we are playing the championship game, and it's our biggest game we have ever played. As we entered Lorelle Park, we noticed the park was packed.

The national anthem starts to play, and the next thing you hear is the umpire saying, let's play ball. The team and I head on the field, and I think how hot it is, but hope for our team is fading fast.

It's now the bottom of the 7th inning, and we trail 6 to 1. Nash is at-bat; he finds a hole and makes it to first base, Josiah makes it to second, Landon walks to the batter box, waits for the pitch, and hits a double, but they tag Nash, giving us our first out.

Next up is Christian; he's our best player. He hits a square up; it goes over second basemen head to left field; unable to catch the ball, Christian gets to first base, Landon is unable to get to third base; he is forced to stay on second base.

Josiah runs home, making the score 6-2. The team is excited, Sean is up, but the Mighty Hawks intentionally walk him.

The bases are loaded, and Ricky, who scored a home run in the 2nd inning, strikes out this time. Back to the batters' box is Aiden; the pitcher throws a fastball, Aiden connects, and he hits a line drive, allowing Landon to run home. The score is 6-3 with two outs,

and the dugout is crazed; it's my turn to bat, I slowly start walking to the batter's box, and a sensation comes over me;

I begin to pray, Please God, please give me the strength to hit this ball. My heart is beating out of my chest, I say to myself, here goes nothing. As the words escape my mouth, I hear the umpire say strike 1, strike 2, strike 3, you're out.

My teammates hung their heads, but no one said anything, and we're back on the field.

The Mighty Hawks score four more runs, and the score is 10-3. Our team feels deflated for the first time in this game. Coach Miller walks over to us and says, we're down 7 runs. Please don't give up now. It's only the bottom of the 8th; let's play this game until it's over.

I began to feel the butterflies in my stomach again; I'm so scared.

The Coach signals for Auden as he enters the box, the first pitch is thrown, the umpire yells, ball, the next pitch is a curveball, Auden connects, and the crowd is on their feet.

Everyone is excited because he brings in Nash; the score is now 10-4. The Mighty Hawks pitcher throws another bender and strikes Ricky out again. Alex says to Ricky, hey Buddy, don't get in a slump.

Alex is in the batter's box; he swings and makes it to first base, the whole team is standing, and you can feel the excitement in the park.

Michael yells! We have a chance now, as we all jump for joy. Everyone in the dugout believes this until the coach calls for me (MJ) to bat.

The dugout goes silent, and then I hear my very own private cheerleading squad yelling, MJ! you got this! My Mom begins to chat home run, home run; we want a home run. I leisurely pick up my bat; I begin to pray, God, please let me bring in one player, just one player, please God.

24

The crowd starts to clap uncontrollably, but it quiets down when they hear the umpire say ball one, the pitcher re-adjusts, then I hear strike one, strike two, the noise in the park intensifies, I'm not sure what to do;

when I hear the coach say run MJ run! I take off running and then trip, I immediately get up, I make it to third base and I'm even more excited because Landon, Alex, and Auden all make it home. My heart is about to burst open with joy, as I realize, I just hit my first triple! (smiling)

The score is now 10-7: the stadium has come alive, and Jaden, our cleanup batter, is up next. The pitcher throws a fastball, Jaden swings; he hits the ball, and it's a line drive, allowing me to run in, but he's out. The crowd is profoundly loud, and I feel like I'm on the Yankees team (smiling).

Now it's 10-8 with two outs, Sean is at-bat and the Mighty Hawks deliberately walk him again; next up to bat is Preston, we leap out of the dugout; it's the second home run for the Blue Bears, and the game is tied. We are genuinely excited, we go into overtime, but the Mighty Hawks get two more runs and win the game 12-10.

The Coach hugs us all, tells us how proud he is of the team, and asks if we're ready to celebrate? We all yelled yes! With excitement, the Coach then tells us, he will meet us at Henry's for pizza in 30 minutes.

When the Coach walks in, the team and parents all stand and give him a standing ovation. He says thank you, but we didn't win the championship, as the smile on his face becomes more prominent. But it sure does feel like it, as his smile gets wider.

The team is emotional, and we begin to clap; we hug each other with delight. 30 minutes have passed, as we continue to eat, the Coach stands and expresses his gratitude once more to the team. He tells us that he's proud of the hard work, dedication, and respect that we displayed to one another as teammates.

He then says, what a season, and with great pride, he says, MJ, what a hit! I beamed with pure joy. Later that night, my mom reminds me to say my prayers as she always does, and I can't wait to thank God.

As I began to say my prayers, I remembered a question Mr. Evans, my bible school teacher asked years ago in class. The question he asked the class was, is God real? Has anyone in this class ever felt God? Will you know what God feels like when he's with you? Do you believe in God?

Well, I didn't understand the question then, but I do now; It was like a lightning bolt that struck me.

I'm 12 years old, and my first experience with God was in a playoff game between the Mighty Hawk and Blue Bears. I prayed to God and asked him to help me, and he did.

Mr. Evans once said that God is happy when we're afraid because we call on him when we need help, and he was right; I was so scared, I didn't want to let the team down.

The only thing I could think to do in the 7th and 8th inning was pray. At that very moment, I knew that God was real and that I loved God and that He loved me. Is God real to you? The End.

Printed in the United States
by Baker & Taylor Publisher Services